STEPHEN F. AUSTIN

Stories

For Young

Americans

Stephen F.

Austin

The Father

Of

Texas

By Jean Flynn

EAKIN PRESS ★ AUSTIN, TEXAS

FIRST EDITION
Second Printing

Copyright © 1981
By Jean Flynn

Published in the United States of America
By Eakin Press, P.O. Box 23066, Austin, Texas 78735

ISBN 1-57168-567-7

For Deirdre Siobhan

TABLE OF CONTENTS

FOREWORD

There are many stories surrounding Stephen F. Austin. His name is more widely repeated than any other Texas hero. Yet, few students can remember his personality or anything specific about his life. He was not flashy nor dramatic in his actions. His emotions were well hidden except for those with whom he corresponded.

I am gratefully indebted to Eugene C. Barker who collected and published the Austin papers. The letters quoted in this biography are direct quotes from the letters contained in Dr. Barker's works. I have tried to interpret the letters within the historical times in which they were written. I hope I have captured the essence of the man, Stephen F. Austin.

Jean Flynn

I

THE AUSTIN FAMILY

"Boom!" The wooden two-storied house shook with each shot fired. Stephen looked down from his hiding place on the stairs. He stuck his small, pale face between the banister to look below. Excitement and fear filled his small body while he watched the men fire their long barreled muzzle-loaders. Darkness surrounded the house. Each time the rifles were fired flashes of light momentarily lit up the faces of the men. He heard the yelps of the Indians when they attacked again and again.

"Stephen," cried Emily from the bedroom. "Where are you?"

"Shhh," Stephen whispered. "Stop crying. Mama will hear you."

Emily did not hear him above the roar of the muzzle-loaders below. "Stephen!" she screamed.

Their mother looked up from hurrying to carry ammunition to her husband. She quickly gave him the gun powder. Frowning, she ran up the stairs and dragged Stephen into the bedroom.

"I told you to stay with your little sister," she scolded him.

"But Mama, I am big enough to help the men," he said proudly.

1

Mrs. Austin wrapped her arms around Emily. "You musn't be afraid. You have your big brother to keep you safe," she said. Then she pulled Stephen close to her. "You are a brave boy. Watch Emily for me and stay away from the window. If you see fire or smell smoke, call me at once."

Stephen sat in the corner between a chair and the wall. Emily sat quietly beside him. Oh, he wished he could fight with the men. When the thirty or more Indians attacked his home, he had begged to help. He knew that he was smaller than the other eight-year-old boys in the village, but he was strong.

The night was long and dark. Stephen stayed awake and watched the window. Emily cried herself to sleep. Sometime in the darkness of the night, Stephen laid her head on his lap.

Finally the room began to cast shadows with the morning sun. The gunshots became fewer and fewer. Mrs. Austin came to tell the children that the Indians had gone. She found Emily asleep. Stephen was still watching the window.

The Indian attack on October 12, 1802, was typical of Stephen Fuller Austin's life. He was never involved in the dramatic fights in the history of Texas. Yet he is more widely known than any other Texas hero. He always stood strong through the long vigils of the night.

Stephen's patience was not inherited from his father. Where he was tactful and fair-spoken, Moses was abrupt and harsh. Father and son were different in every way except in their loyalty to Texas. Moses recognized Stephen's strength as a diplomat. He shaped his son for leadership. More often than not, Stephen helped his father to deal with one business failure after another.

Unlike Stephen, Moses often took risks. He built one business after another to fall always into debt. He began work in a dry goods store when he was fourteen. By the time he was twenty, he was in business with his brother-in-law. At the age of twenty-three, he expanded his dry goods business from Philadelphia to Richmond. By 1784, he was exporting dry goods from England.

In 1785, when he was twenty-four, he felt he was wealthy enough to marry. He married Maria Brown, daughter of a wealthy Philadelphia merchant. They made their home in Richmond, Virginia. Everything looked bright for Moses and Maria. Moses was making money. They lived in the largest house in Richmond. Maria had many servants.

Then sadness fell upon their household. Two daughters were born to them. Both lived only a few months. Moses became unhappy with his life as a merchant.

In 1791, Moses and Maria began their westward movement. They moved to the lead mines in Wythe County, Virginia. It was a time of gigantic land speculation in western lands. Many wealthy men bought land while the price was cheap. When the land began to develop and was valuable, the owners sold the property for a huge profit.

Moses knew the soil and the character of the lands. Speculators, men who had money to invest in lands, paid him to invest their money. He located the land, surveyed the boundries, and purchased it for them.

Moses built up a settlement in Wythe County, Virginia. The settlement was named Austinville. For a time the Austins were happy again. Their happiness seemed complete when their first son was born. Stephen Fuller Austin was born in Austinville on November 3, 1793.

No one knows why Moses did not succeed in his business. But once again he failed. Money was scarce in those days. Business was often done by credit and barter. Moses was not a conservative businessman. He found himself in debt beyond his means to pay.

When Stephen was three years old, Moses and Maria began their second westward movement. Moses learned of rich lead deposits in southwestern Missouri. He decided to explore the land.

The land with the rich mines was under Spanish rule. Baron Carondelet, governor of Louisiana, encouraged generous land grants to settlers. He wanted Americans to settle the land to form a barrier against the British Canadians.

Although Carondelet had a keen appreciation for the frontiersmen, he wanted families to settle the land. He knew the frontiersmen could survive great difficulties.

The frontiersman traveled with only a carbine and a little sack of cornmeal. With the carbine he killed his game for meat and clothes. He protected himself against savage Indians. Mixing a little water with his cornmeal, he made bread. When he needed shelter, he stacked logs in a square, criss-crossing the corners. He stuck mud and grass in the cracks between the logs to make snug walls. The roof was made from long branches cut from the logs.

The problem was that the frontiersmen did not stay in one place. Whey they got restless, they simply moved on. Carondelet wanted Americans who would stay rooted. When Moses Austin set out on a cold day, December 8, 1796, he had a good chance of getting his land grant.

Moses, dressed for the cold, long trip, headed toward St. Louis. He had to cross many streams that were frozen over. On his way he met many people moving to Kentucky. Their poverty was sad. Whole families traveled together. Many were half clothed in rags and barefooted on the ice and snow. They were nearly starved to death, but they would not stop.

Moses talked to some of the families. They were passing over land as rich in soil as they would find in Kentucky. They would not listen. Kentucky was the promised land that would fulfill their dreams. Many could not survive the hardships. Those who could not go on died. They didn't have the strength to return to their homes.

Moses thought about the nature of man who would suffer such conditions to obtain his dream. But wasn't that what he was doing? It took him forty-eight days of hardships and cold to arrive at St. Louis.

He wasted no time after he arrived. He gathered influential and moneyed men to go into his venture. He wanted the land around and including Mine á Burton.

The mine, located forty miles west of St. Louis, was just what he thought it would be. It covered forty acres. The lead deposits were more plentiful and of better quality than any he had ever seen.

No one lived around the mine. All of the miners lived at St. Genevieve. They worked as a group from August to November. The Osage Indians were very hostile. The miners were afraid of them.

Moses was excited. The mine belonged to the Spanish government but was subject to grant. He once again gathered the men who would support his venture. Partnerships in the mine were formed. An application for the grant was presented and approved.

A happy Moses Austin returned to Missouri. He quickly organized a work group to return to the mines. Much work was to be done before lead could be sold. Furnaces had to be built. A shaft into the mine had to be sunk. A saw mill had to be erected on the land. And a factory had to be ready in St. Genevieve to take the raw lead.

Moses sold all of his business holdings. Finally, on June 8, 1798, the Austin party began another move. Forty people began the trip. It was a frightening trip for five-year-old Stephen. The party left Austinville in wagons. No one could go far from the group because of savage Indians. Stephen always had to stay close to his mother. Emily, his sister, was only three. She cried more than he did. She wanted to sit on his mother's lap. Stephen wanted to ride in the front of the wagon with his father. He was afraid because he had to lie flat and be covered up most of the time.

They left the wagons with settlers on the bank of the Kanawha River. The barge they loaded was fairly large. Stephen was tied by a short rope most of the trip so he could not fall into the rough waters. He heard the women scream when two men fell overboard and were swept away in the muddy water. He heard them cry when his uncle died.

There were very few settlements along the river. The land was untamed. The Indians were wild and savage. Stephen did not understand everything that was happening. He was intelligent and sensitive enough to know that something was drastically wrong.

Only seventeen of the forty people in the party arrived safely. Of the seventeen only two had enough strength to walk ashore without help. This was only the first difficulty that Moses had in his new venture.

Mine á Burton was located in land where boundaries had not been marked. There was fighting over who had the first claim to the land. Moses was not an easy man to deal with. He acted too quickly and spoke too bluntly.

Moses overcame the hardships of the first year. In 1799, his business was once again prospering. He operated the mine year around. He moved his family to a new house at Mine á Burton. It was at this house in 1802 that the Indians attacked Moses and his family. Ten working men helped Moses drive them away.

A village grew up around the mine. Supplies for the

village were needed. Moses opened a store where he sold clothing material, household and kitchen furniture, hardware, lead products, and country produce.

As the little colony around the square grew, so did Stephen. He helped his father in the store. He was content in his belief that this was where he would spend his youth. He enjoyed listening to all of the scary tales of the men who came to the store. At last his family was settled. He never wanted to leave.

II

A RELUCTANT STUDENT

"But I don't want to go away to school," Stephen argued with his father. Still small for his age and not as robust as his father, he stood his ground. He liked working in the store and hearing all of the stories told by the men who traded there.

"You are eleven years old. It is time to think of your education," Moses Austin stated firmly. "You will go."

"Why do I have to go and Emily doesn't?" Stephen was bold enough to ask.

Moses looked at his son's stubborn face. "Because you are older than Emily. Your sister will go when it *is* time."

Moses loved his family. He wanted the best for them. Although the colony around the mine had grown, he was concerned for his children's education. There were now three children. Another son, James Elijah Brown Austin was born to them the year before on October 3, 1803.

As Moses talked to Stephen, he remembered his own childhood. He wanted better things for his children. It was now safe for Stephen to travel to Connecticut. He must go to Bacon Academy.

In May, 1804, as the sun rose to bring warmth to the

cold earth, Stephen began his trip. Daniel Phelps was traveling through the colony on his way to Conneticut. He would be Stephen's escort.

Excitement began to grow inside the small boy. His pale face was pink. His eyes sparkled. Since he had to do as his father wished, he hoped something exciting would happen on the trip. He waved bravely to his family until they were out of sight on the shore.

He watched the shoreline for Indians. He saw none. He hoped for rough waters to shake the boat. The river was smooth. But he never gave up his watch during the long, uncomfortable trip to Conneticut.

Stephen often became homesick for his family in the early days at Bacon Academy. Many times he hid his tears from his friends. He was a boarder with the John Adams family during most of his three years there.

Dr. Adams was the preceptor or principal of Bacon Academy. He was a good teacher. He was strict, but he was gentle and kind. Stephen was happy with the Adams family. They treated him like he was part of the family.

Even from afar, Moses directed Stephen's education. He wrote his instructions to Dr. Adams. He wanted Stephen to be a scholar, but he saw no reason for him to study Greek and Hebrew. He did not want Stephen to be encouraged to be a religious scholar. He wanted Stephen to gain a business sense. If his son had the talent, Moses wanted him to study law. Dr. Adams was to instruct Stephen on how to write well and to teach him "a correct mode of thinking." He also wanted Stephen to be trained in music if "he has a mind that way."

Moses also set down a code of conduct for Stephen in his first letter to his son.

I charge you to write every month...You made three Black marks at the close of your letter and put your name on the left hand side of the paper, this is wrong, always put your name as near the right side of the paper as you can...

Stephen blinked away tears when he read the letter. He wasn't angry with his father. He could see mistakes in his father's letter. He didn't even mind that. He just wanted to be home with his family.

Stephen accepted the way his father wrote. Moses was blunt. He didn't mean to hurt his son. He wanted Stephen to succeed. The young Stephen tried to fulfill his father's ideals. He studied hard. His classmates helped him to develop refined social graces. He learned to appreciate good music. Overcoming his shyness, he learned to dance and loved it. His writing was some of the most literary of the day. He grew into a young man with a liberal mind. He had dreams of achieving greatness.

The three years he spent at Bacon Academy passed quickly. He graduated with honors. His teachers praised him as being an outstanding scholar. The residents of Cholchester liked and respected him.

Moses had wanted Stephen to study law at Yale. That dream was not fulfilled. Moses was once again suffering financial problems.

Moses had sent Emily to a boarding school in Lexington, Kentucky. He now had the expense of education for two children. There were many problems at the mine. Currency was scarce. Little money, if any, passed hands. Moses was falling more and more into debt.

At the age of fourteen, Stephen crossed the mountains and entered Transylvania University. Located at Lexington, Kentucky, it was the first university of the West.

Some of his classmates were very bright students. Many nights were spent in deep discussions. Stephen was a thinker. He was excited by people as interested in politics as he was. His classmates liked and respected his opinions. The young men did not spend all of their time in studies. There was a lightheartedness about them also. They went to parties. Stephen loved to dance. He flirted with the girls. He took young ladies for Sunday afternoon walks. His friends teased him when he visited the same girl twice.

On April 10, 1810, he gradutate from Transylvania University with honors. His formal education had ended. The family finances could not stand the burden of sending him to law school. He was asked to return to Missouri. His father needed him to help with the businesses. Stephen returned home.

A boy, yet a man, stood on the bank of the river in the fall of 1810. He looked longingly at the barge nearby. Stephen waved to his mother, Emily, and James as the barge slowly moved away. They were going East. Emily was to go to a finishing school. James, now eight years old, was to study with Reverend Samuel Whittlesy.

Stephen Fuller Austin's worries had just begun. His carefree life was in the past. Never again would he be free from responsibility to others. The Austin family struggled from one financial failure to another.

Maria Austin ran out of money. She was constantly embarrassed by having to bargain for credit. Her husband was thought to be wealthy. She was expected to dress according to her social standing. There were bills to keep up appearances. There was no money to send to her.

In 1812, Moses loaded a cargo of lead and put Stephen in charge of it. He was to go to the East and sell the lead. The eastern prices were high. The one cargo would put everything right for Mrs. Austin.

Stephen knew the importance of the trip. He also knew the dangers involved. The boat was heavy with its cargo of lead. Navigation would be difficult. The waters in the Mississippi River shifted from one pass to another. Steamers often had difficulty getting through to deep water. There were snags under the muddy water that he would have to avoid.

With a great deal of anxiety, Stephen began his slow trip. He had memorized the instructions from his father. Never run late at night. Never stop under a high bank and large trees. Never trust the boat to float unless there is a man on lookout. Tie the boat securely at night with a strong cable. Always put to land in winds. Keep out of the bends of the rivers.

Stephen guarded his cargo carefully. He followed his father's instructions. He slept only when the boat was secure for the night.

He was greatly saddened by what he saw along the shore of the river. Many villages were in ruins. After the great earthquake in February of that year, many settlers were left in poverty once again. They did not have the heart to rebuild what the earthquake had destroyed. Surely, Stephen thought, there is a place where man can build on his dreams and prosper.

The trip was uneventful for several days. The boat ran into waters flowing fast and furious, but Stephen reached the Mississippi River with no real problems. The Ohio River had been blue and clear. The Mississippi River was dark brown.

The boat had been in the muddy waters for several days when the accident happened. It hit a snag under the surface of the swirling, muddy water. The boat creaked and groaned under the weight of the heavy, lead cargo. Water gushed through a hole in the boat. It began to sink quickly.

Stephen was helpless. There was no way he could keep the boat from sinking. He hurried the crew into small boats. They all escaped unharmed. Stephen watched with dismay as the boat shuddered when it hit the muddy bottom of the river.

For weeks Stephen worked to recover the lead. When he eventually got to New Orleans, the War of 1812 had begun. Trade was almost stopped. He sold the lead at a loss and returned to Missouri. He felt that he had failed the first important job his father had given him.

The Austins could no longer afford to keep up the pretense of wealth. Maria, Emily, and James returned from the East. Stephen vowed never to marry until his family was cleared of debts. He never married.

Moses believed that lack of currency was causing many problems. Money rarely was seen. In 1816, he, along with several businessmen, applied to the territorial legislature for authority to establish a bank. Their request was granted. The bank opened for business before the year ended.

Earlier that same year Moses moved Maria from Mine á Burton. Emily was happily married. James was once again away at school. Stephen, twenty-two years old, took over Durham Hall Plantation and the mine. He was determined to "free the family from every embarrassment."

Misfortune fell again. The great depression of 1818-1819 struck everywhere. Moses declared bankruptcy. Even land which Stephen had bought in Arkansas turned out to have a defective title.

The only success in which Stephen felt secure was his political career. He was elected to the House of Representatives in 1814. He often questioned his business ability. He never questioned his political sense. He was a true representative of the people who elected him. He was re-elected yearly for four years. Stephen Fuller Austin was gaining valuable experience for his life as a Texan.

III

THE TEXAS DREAM

"Texas is the place to begin again," Moses said.

Stephen looked at his father. He thought his father had grown old quickly. He did not know when the idea of a Texas settlement first began with Moses. Virginia, Missouri, and Arkansas had failed the Austin family. Moses rugged face showed his disappointment.

Unlike his father, Stephen was patient, methodical, energetic, and fair-spoken. He knew the types of frontiersmen who mingled in the newly opened land. Moses did not intend to encourage the frontiersmen. The type of settlement he wanted included families. Stephen decided to help his father so he could then get on with his own life.

Unknown to Stephen, he was at the beginning of his lifelong career. He was twenty-seven years old. He was well-educated for his day. He was experienced in public service and business. And he felt a strong family loyalty.

Stephen opened a farm on the bed of Red River in 1819. The farm was to be the resting place for emigrants. It was also to be a base for supplies to help the settlers in the Texas wilderness. After investigating the route into Texas, Stephen decided the best way was through New

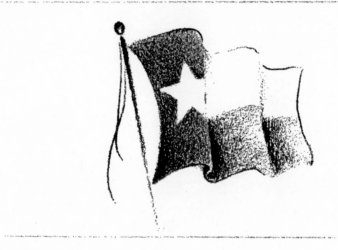

Orleans or Natchitoches. The farm on Red River was abandoned.

Stephen met his father in Little Rock, Arkansas, to plan the settlement. In November, 1820, Moses headed toward San Antonio de Bexar which was then under Spanish rule. Stephen left for New Orleans to make arrangements for settlers who wanted to move to Texas.

Moses had had to borrow money from Stephen to make the trip. He had a gray horse, a mule, a black slave, and fifty dollars in cash. He insisted that Stephen make out a note which said that Moses was to return the possessions or pay $850. Stephen was not repaid. He had not expected to be.

Bexar was just what Moses expected. There was excitement about the town. He felt the happiness of Christmas when he arrived on December 23, 1820. His expectations were high.

Governor Antonio María Martinez was not kind. Moses was treated as if he were on trial. In answer to the questions asked of him, he stated that he was a Catholic and a subject of Spain. He wished to settle his family in Texas and cultivate cotton, corn, and sugar.

He had no goods to trade. He had been prompted by the liberal policy of Spain to move to Texas. He wished to settle three hundred families who had the same desires as he did.

Governor Antonio María Martinez listened to Moses' answers. He had a frown on his face. Without explaining why, he said, "You will leave Bexar immediately. If you do not remove yourself from the province of Texas as quickly as your horse will carry you, you will be placed under arrest."

The shock on his face turned to despair as Moses crossed the plaza. There was nothing to do but gather his few possessions from his rented room. The happy games of the children playing in the park brought no joy to his saddened heart.

"Is that you, Moses Austin?" a man asked him. Moses raised his eyes to the first friendly face he had seen since going into the governor's office. Baron de Bastrop, a friend from Louisiana, shook his hand.

The Baron had been in Bexar for fifteen years. He knew all of the influential people. He was well-liked. At one time he had been given permission to begin a settlement. The colony was never established.

When Moses explained his disappointment to him, the Baron immediately set out to help him. He talked to Governor Martinez. Moses was allowed to stay in Bexar. The Baron presented the application to settle families for Moses.

Governor Martinez considered the application for three days. Then, for some unknown reason, he approved it. He immediately sent it on to the commandant general of Eastern Interior Provinces of Spain.

Moses was once again certain that his grant would be approved. He did not wait for an answer. By January 15th, he was back at McGuffin's place, a noted landmark between Natchitoches and the Sabine River. Hugh McGuffin's farm had become a resting place for weary travelers.

Moses was ill when he arrived there. He had suffered many hardships in the cold weather. His pack animals had been stolen. His gunpowder had become too wet to fire. He and his servant had struggled eight days to survive. He was in bed for three weeks before he was strong enough to continue his trip home. Texas had become his dream. He saw the Texas settlement as a way to regain his lost fortunes. He was a proud man. He could no longer live in poverty where he had once been wealthy.

His dream gave him the strength to return home and

begin his new venture. A tired and ill man arrived home in March, 1821. He gained new strength when he learned that his grant had been approved.

He was enthusiastic and began planning. He had been granted 200,000 acres of land for three hundred families. The terms of the grant were vague. He believed that he could make his own terms with the settlers.

Moses wrote to Stephen. The grant had been officially approved on January 17th. Although he was tired and ill, he wrote, they must start promoting the settlement. He knew that he could count on Stephen's help. This venture was the greatest and most important undertaking of his life. It must succeed.

While Moses was petitioning for the land grant, Stephen was trying to make a place for himself. He was penniless. He had not been trained for any one job or position. Politics and law were his interests. He saw in law as a profession a way of making money. He wanted to pay off the debts he had made when he was in his father's business. He wanted to relieve his mother of financial worry.

With a great deal of thought and planning, Stephen began his law studies in January, 1821. He became a clerk to Joseph H. Hawkins. He worked in exchange for his room and board and being taught law by Hawkins. Hawkins loaned him law books to study and some money for necessary clothes.

He soon acquired a second job. He earned extra money as the assistant editor of the *Louisiana Advertiser*. Hawkins recognized Stephen's ability to write well. He encouraged Stephen to use that talent.

Stephen was impressed with Hawkins. He felt at last he had found where he belonged. He wrote to his mother that he would be able to send her money after eighteen months. He hoped he could begin paying off debts before the people he owed began prosecuting him. He had many dreams about his future. He saw those dreams as being a reality when he became a lawyer.

Once again Stephen's plans were changed by his father. He had been concerned about his father's health since receiving Moses' letter that the land grant had been approved. Now Maria wrote her son that his father was gravely ill. He had never fully recovered from his trip to Texas.

Tears came to his eyes while he read and re-read his mother's letter. Moses had begged her from his sickbed to write to Stephen. Stephen must carry on his work for the Texas settlement.

Stephen was pulled between two desires. He wanted to become a lawyer. He also wanted to help his father. But he didn't want to spend his life in his father's shadow. He must decide quickly.

A letter from James, his brother, decided Stephen's choice. James urged him that the mission was important not only to their father but to the settler and Texas.

On June 18, 1821, Stephen left New Orleans to carry on his father's work. Mr. Hawkins agreed with Stephen's decision. He also helped to finance the colonization. Mr. Hawkins would keep him informed about his father's health.

With a party of eight to ten men, Stephen began his journey. He met Juan José María de Jesús Seguin, who had been sent by Governor Martinez to escort Moses. They were to explore the province of the colonization contract on their way to Bexar.

The men were breaking camp on July 10, 1821, when they heard the sound of horses hooves. It sounded like only one rider. A messenger jumped from a lathered horse and asked, ''Is Stephen Austin among you?''

Stephen stepped forward just as the sun peeked over

the horizon. He knew before he read the message. His father was dead. As he looked at the men gathered around the campground, the sadness in his eyes told them the news. He walked away. He wanted to be alone to think.

He knew better than anyone else what his father had dreamed. Texas was open country. It had rich land. Many families could begin a new life. He had the ability to work between the people and the Spanish government. His knowledge of law would help him to write sound contracts.

He straightened his shoulders and looked at the fertile land that was Texas. He would continue his father's dream. The burden of colonization now rested on his shoulders. Colonization must not fail. "In this," he said to himself, "I will succeed."

IV

TEXAS COLONIZATION BEGINS

Stephen watched the eager faces while he explained the colonization laws. A group of thirty-six had gathered at the first meeting in Nacogdoches. The sun was hot on that July day in 1821. No one seemed to care. They were ready to move onto the Austin grant.

Colonization had begun. Stephen appointed James Hill as temporary head of the settlement. He wanted this group united in their efforts. Someone needed to be in charge while he was away. He needed to continue his trip to Bexar with Seguin.

Seguin had notified Governor Martinez that Moses was dead. His son Stephen had taken the resposiblity of completing the agreement. Seguin asked Martinez to provide good quarters for Stephen and his men.

When the group arrived on August 12, the governor recognized Stephen as heir to his father's commitments. He gave Stephen permission to explore the lands on the Colorado River.

Stephen agreed to follow the orders of the government of Spain. The settlement could bring provisions, tools, and farming equipment duty free through the port of San Bernard. Stephen agreed to be responsible for the good character of the immigrants. Until the government could organize the local administration, the settlers were under Stephen's rule.

He left Bexar with a light heart. The next step he had planned was to notify the public about his grant. He went directly to New Orleans. He published a pamphlet stating colonization requirements.

While Stephen was organizing his colony, the Spaniards and Mexicans were at war. The Mexican revolutionists swept the Spanish out of power. Stephen had to stop his work and go to Mexico City for permission to continue his colony under Mexican rule.

He worried about the trip. He had very little money. The Indians were a constant menace. Beyond Monterrey the country swarmed with bandits. But he had no choice. He must get approval for his colony.

He gathered a group of experienced men to go with him. The small traveling party had been warned of the dangers. They watched the trail closely for signs of fresh hoof prints. They listened carefully for someone approaching them. At night they took turns standing guard over the horses and the campground.

Day after day they rode without seeing any signs or hearing any sounds of danger. They did not see or hear the Indians when they realized they were surrounded. A group of about fifty Comanches seemed to appear from nowhere. They were on all sides of the travelers.

There was nothing the group of white men could do. Stephen slowly shook his head to warn the men that they should not resist. The Comanches seemed to recognize him as the leader. He and his men remained quiet while the Indians took all of their possessions. Their heartbeats quickened as the Comanches talked among themselves.

The white men sensed an argument among them. They could not understand the Indians' language. The

24

sounds of their voices told the frightened group that the Indians were exchanging angry words. Then the Indians looked the Americans over severely.

No one moved. An older Indian brave began returning the stolen property. The Comanches parted and made way for the Americans to ride away. "Hold back. Hold back," Stephen warned. "Do not run." The sound of their horses' hooves seemed to echo as they moved slowly on their way. The Indians disappeared as quickly and quietly as they had appeared.

When the traverlers stopped to check their property, they found the Indians had not returned everything. Four blankets were missing.

"They didn't return my spare bridle," said the guide for the party.

"Well, if we all study Spanish, maybe we can talk to them next time," Stephen laughed, "because they kept my Spanish grammar book!"

The rest of the trip was uneventful, but Stephen felt the nervous strain of waiting for something to happen. He was despondent when they arrived in Mexico City on April 29, 1822.

He knew no one. He felt ignorant of the language and the laws. The government was totally different in character from the one he knew. He had very little money. His hope was that he would get approval for his colonization quickly.

With each postponement for approval, Stephen wrote to Texas that he hoped to return in ten days. But each ten days turned into weeks of delay. For seven months he worked patiently to have his grant approved.

The Mexican government was in a turmoil. No one would take the responsibility of passing the colonization law. Each article of Stephen's proposal was discussed and voted on from the amount of land to be awarded each family to the problem of slavery.

By the time the grant passed legislation, Stephen had sold his watch for money to live. But the legislation passed a general act. He still had to go to the emperor for the grant to be confirmed. He was in financial straits. For four months he lived on borrowed money. He lived meagerly. His clothes were worn thin. But he completed his work. He was pleased that the Mexican officials praised him for his patience and energy. He had become a respected and influential man among them.

He left the city on April 18, 1823. He had been gone a year. During that time he had truly become a Mexican citizen. Within four months of his arrival, he had been speaking and writing Spanish. That won him the confidence of the Mexican officials. They now called him "Estevan," the Spanish name for Stephen. As he rode away from the city, he pledged himself to fulfill all obligations as a Mexican citizen.

His success in Mexico City was soon forgotten when he arrived back in Texas and faced the problems of the colonists. In his long absence, confusion by the colonists led to many rumors. There was suspense about land titles. The Indians were hostile to the settlers. The severe drought destroyed the corn crops. The colonists had to eat deer and wild horses.

As the news of the troubles of the settlers traveled back to the United States, the stories were exaggerated out of proportion. There were reports that Stephen F. Austin had drowned. One rumor was that he was killed by hostile Indians. A group of half-crazed immigrants trying to return to the United States told Hugh McGuffin that they could testify that Austin was actually dead.

The unrest among the settlers caused problems. Two groups had been formed by the end of 1822. The settlements were widely separated. One was on the Colorado

River. The second was on the Brazos River.

Baron de Bastrop had become the colony's land commissioner when Mexico took over Texas. In Stephen's absence, he had gathered the colonists on the Colorado. He assured them that their land grants were safe. He encouraged them to unite against the Tonkawa and Karankawa Indians.

The settlers pledged their allegiance to Mexico. They chose an alcalde, a captain, and a lieutenant. Bastrop left the settlement in good spirits. He sent Josiah H. Bell to do the same thing with the settlement on the Brazos.

The satisfaction of the colonists was short lived. No rules had been given the alcaldes. They worked out a rough system of their own, probably based on their knowledge of the United States judicial system. The office of alcalde was not a comfortable one. They had only public opinion to support their decisions. They lived in constant fear of offending some unfamiliar Mexican custom.

Immigration to the Austin settlements had practically stopped when he returned from Mexico. He immediately set out to stop all rumors. Accompanied by Baron de Bastrop, he went to the Colorado settlement. Bastrop again spoke to the gathering. Stephen F. Austin was to have authority as supreme civil, judicial, and military authority.

Two days later, Austin issued a statement. The legality of the grant was now unquestionable. The titles to the land would be secure forever. Success of the settlements depended on the hardihood, unity, determination, and willingness of the colonists to be guided by him. He desired their prosperity almost as much as he did for his own family.

Austin began to deal with two pressing problems to restore the confidence of the settlers. Surveys of land and titles must be issued as quickly as possible. The second

27

problem involved the hostile Indians hovering around the settlements. Somehow, he must put the fear of the white man in the minds of the Indians.

He made a contract with Seth Ingram to survey the Colorado immediately. His first step to combat the Indians was to form a group of rangers. He employed ten men under the command of Lieutenant Moses Morrison.

Then Austin set about checking the settlements. He was on the Brazos in September when the Tonkawas made a raid on the settlement. He quickly gathered thirty men and followed the Indians to their camp.

The men were afraid when Austin rode straight into the Indians' campground. The Indians were surprised at his bravery. Fear crossed their eyes as Austin rode his horse right up to the chief.

"You will return all of the stolen horses," he demanded. There was quiet talk among the Indians. He waited silently for the talk to stop and then ordered the chief, "You will whip the braves who have done this bad thing. If any thieves are caught in the future, they will be killed."

A flicker of fear came into the chief's eyes and he nodded his head that he understood. Without another word, Austin turned his horse and rode slowly from the camp.

During the night, the settlers heard the quiet sounds of movement around their houses. They had bolted the doors and stood guard in case of an Indian attack. The next morning they found their horses grazing peacefully in their yards. The Tonkawa tribe had about one hundred and fifty members. They were too weak to resist against the settlers. Austin's threat frightened them. In May, 1824, a treaty was signed that the Indians would stay out of the settlement.

The Coaques and the Karankawas were more difficult

to handle. Austin believed them to be universal enemies to man. They killed off everyone who fell within their powers. Frequently they feasted on the bodies of their victims. Austin believed the tribes would have to be exterminated.

His belief almost proved true. The first organized movement against the tribes began in June, 1824. Captain Robert Kuykendall asked Austin for a detachment of militia to fight. Kuykendall believed the Indians would retreat against a formed group. The Indians and the rangers fought several battles. No one won. The Indians seemed to know where the rangers were and were always prepared for them.

Austin became angered by the Indians' open hositility. He formed a group of sixty-two men to hunt down the tribe of offenders. When the tribe saw the size of Austin's well-armed group, they retreated. The white men followed relentlessly.

The Indians became afraid and took refuge at the mission at La Bahía. When Austin came within two miles of the town, a priest and the municipal officers met him. They worked out a treaty. The Karankawas promised not to set foot past the San Antonio River.

While protection against the outside forces increasd, the settlers were becoming dissatisfied. The settlers had agreed to pay Austin twelve and a half cents tax per acre of their land allotment. The land grants were very liberal. Many people did not have the money to pay. They believed that Austin was paid for the time and money he spent by the government.

The settlers signed an agreement to the terms before coming to Texas. Criticism began to pass from mouth to mouth about Austin's efforts. People who were not unhappy began questioning his efforts.

In defense of himself, Austin published an address to

the colonists. He retold his father's efforts which cost him his life. He reviewed the terms of the contract. He reminded them of all of his expenses and time spent in Mexico. To prove his good will, he had paid for all land surveys and titles. An administration and militia had been formed for their protection. He begged the colonists to consider the advantages of his working for the betterment of colonization.

Austin believed he was just in his requests. He had accepted any kind of property to cover the tax. The property had to be changeable for money. He often received horses, mules, hogs, cattle, beeswax, furs, homemade cloth, and whatever items he could sell. He did not demand instant payment. Each colonist made his own arrangement to pay the fee.

Austin had received very few payments. He was in debt and penniless. During all of the complaints, he stood steadfast. By his inner strength, understanding, good judgment, and tact, he gradually quieted the turmoil. Many of the men who had complained against him became his lifelong friends.

With the colony protected and unified again, Austin set out to relieve himself of judicial duties. As each district was formed an alcalde and administration officers were elected. In January, 1824, Austin wrote a set of "Instructions and Regulations for the Alcaldes." It was a brief civil and criminal code. It outlined a definite judicial procedure to be followed.

The Austin colony was growing rapidly. Before the end of 1824, the first colony was firmly established. Austin was ready to send for his mother and widowed sister. He wrote them of the hardships and poverty they would have to endure. "Let our motto be economy and plain living."

Austin's Texas family grew larger each day. His personal family grew smaller. His mother died before she could be brought to Texas. His sister remarried and remained in Missouri. His dreams of rescuing his family from an embarrassing situation in Missouri would never be realized.

V

THE COLONISTS UNDER MEXICAN RULE

Three hundred families firmly established in Texas! The conquest of the wilderness had begun. The Indians were no longer a major threat. The crops were abundant. Comfortable cabins were being built to show the permanence of the settlers.

Stephen F. Austin was confident again. On February 4, 1825, he applied for a second land grant. It was approved on May 20th. He had asked for permission to settle another three hundred families. The government gave him permission to settle five hundred families.

Other empresarios saw Austin's success. They applied for land grants for colonization. But emigrants looking toward Texas wanted in Austin's settlements. Austin had a reputation for getting along with the Mexican authorities. His colonists had received actual titles to their lands. They were prospering and making improvements. The Indians had been taught to fear and respect the white man in the settlements. There was security in the growing strength of the colony.

Austin issued a "Regulations" pamphlet for the interested emigrants. He took no chances for criticism for his tax or fee. His fee for settlement was sixty dollars as empresario of the colonists. This flat fee covered his expenses for the services and benefits he gave them. The money could be paid in installments or he would accept exchangeable goods such as horses, cows, or produce.

He demanded a letter of recommendation. No one would be accepted into the Austin colony without a letter from the highest authority of the emigrants' former places of residence. Austin turned no one away because he could not pay the sixty dollar fee. He did refuse men who had no recommendation.

There was no record kept of the number of people in the first three hundred families. With the fast growth of the settlements, Austin appointed Samuel M. Williams as secretary and recorder. The official census in 1828 recorded 2,021 persons in Austin's settlements. By 1831, population had increased to 5,665.

During the years of rapid growth, Austin's energies were unlimited. He worked with the Indians to prevent trouble. "Foreigners" came to him to be shown land. Often he had to translate the law and federal constitution for them. He approved and passed on applications for land grants. He instructed surveyors.

State and federal officials often required him to do investigations which required much time and labor. His friends used him as a purchasing agent and banker. Other empresarios asked his advice.

The colonists asked him to settle disputes among themselves. He made contracts for them. He assumed debts they could not pay. They asked that he control each local government. They even asked that he curb the lawyers who profited by other's misfortune.

Requests for Austin's help came from the United States. There were constant inquiries from emigrants. He was asked to act as guardian over a runaway youth. He had to settle estates of deceased travelers. Frequently he tried to trace a missing person. Often he was asked to collect debts.

The years between 1828 and 1832 were perhaps Austin's happiest years. He was gradually paying his debt. He had been given a large allotment of land at the foot of the mountains on the Colorado. His cousins were gradually moving to Texas, which gave him great pleasure.

Austin no longer dreamed of great wealth. In January, 1833, he wrote to his sister, Emily Perry, that four thousand dollars more would clear him of debt. He wanted a farm next to his family's. He wanted to be free of public care.

The settlers considered Austin their source of knowledge. He was counselor and guide. They looked to him for authority. When everything was going well, they praised him. When there was trouble, they turned critical eyes upon him. He remained stolid in his actions.

Austin resigned himself to critical abuse. He wrote to his cousin and friend, "I have labor to perform and the seed to sow, but my successor will reap the harvest." The hard years were affecting him. He began to look old. The wrinkles on his face became plainer each day.

One of the major criticisms against Austin was that he was too cautious. He believed in Texas as an independent Mexican state. For that to happen, Texas had to adopt Mexican policy and law. Unity among the settlers would protect them. Division would destroy all that had been done.

Austin was loyal to Mexico. He felt by combining governments, the colonists would be a strong state. The Anglo colonists were impatient. They were not happy with the turmoil in Mexican government.

The United States expressed an interest in purchasing Texas. Andrew Jackson's government made several efforts to buy the state from Mexico. Large companies in the

United States began speculating in land. Austin did not want to annex Texas to the United States. Mexican officials became suspicious of the Anglo settlers. They questioned Austin's loyalty to Mexico.

The law of April 6, 1830, was the beginning of the end of Mexican rule over Texas. The law was to stop the westward movement of people from the United States to Texas. Rumors ran riot. The Mexican government was told of men moving into Texas, not to settle but to revolutionize. There were stories of troops from the United States moving to the frontier. All talk was centered on President Jackson, who was going to take possession of Texas. Newspapers in the United States carried advertisements of forty-eight million acres of land to be settled.

Austin declared himself a Mexican citizen. He was respected by the Mexican officials. He remained neutral and encouraged the colonists to do the same. He advised them to "play the turtle, head and feet within your own shell."

The settled colonists had good deeds to their lands. Their farms were prospering. Their families were growing. They turned from the larger government problems to their own concerns. One of the most important issues concerned religion.

There were no ministers, priests, or preachers, among them. They were married by civil court. The Catholic Church did not consider these marriages binding by law. Many of the settlers were married after moving into the colony. They were worried that the children born to these marriages would not be recognized as legal heirs to their parents' property.

Austin believed in religious toleration. But one of the rules for colonization was to uphold the Catholic religion. He succeeded in getting Father Michael Muldoon to come to his colony in the spring of 1831.

Father Muldoon made a vivid impression on the settlers. He was intelligent and kind. Although he believed strongly in his church, he was very liberal in his thinking. He had a keen sense of humor. He quickly set about marrying the settlers. Then he lined up their children and baptized them.

Father Muldoon's good sense and tact reassured the colonists. They were not persecuted for their lack of belief in the Catholic Church. They hoped one day to have Protestant preachers in their communities. But they did not encourage establishing Protestant churches. The Mexican law of all citizens being Catholic remained.

Religious freedom was not the only concern of the settlers. The Mexican government was trying to do away with slavery in Texas. Most of the colonists owned slaves. The colonists argued that there were no field hands available if they did not own their own slaves. The crops would rot in the fields.

Austin was able to obtain permission for new settlers to bring slaves when they settled land. Any children born to those slaves were to be free at the age of fourteen. After many debates in the legislature, Texas became exempt from the Mexican rule of no slavery.

The exemption did not last. The new colonization law of 1832 restricted slavery. No new slaves could be brought into Texas. The ones already there were to be put on a labor contract of ten years. At the end of the contracts, the slaves were to be set free.

The settlers were furious. In October, 1832, a convention was held. They chose Austin as president of the convention. The settlers wanted Texas to be independent of Coahuila. They wanted to establish a state government. They wrote a petition to present to the Mexican government.

When the Mexicans heard about the convention, they were very unhappy. The officials reminded the colonists that the meeting was unlawful. Santa Anna, temporary president of Mexico, saw the convention as an act of independence. He spoke of his suspicions to the government officials. His pronouncement weakened Austin's position among the Mexican authorities.

Austin convinced the colonists that they should remain calm. The petition was not presented. Calmness did not last long. A new convention was called April 1, 1833.

The second convention did not meet to petition the government. They met to write a state constitution. The leadership in the second convention had changed from the angry colonists who had met before. A newcomer to Texas, Sam Houston, was now a leader.

Houston was from Tennessee. He wasn't a legal resident of Texas. But from the time of his arrival in Texas, people looked up to him. He was a big man, a handsome man. He spoke with authority. The colonists listened to him. And Sam Houston wanted Texas to become a part of the United States.

Houston led the convention in adopting a proposed constitution. The delegates listened to Houston and followed his lead. But they begged Austin to go to Mexico City to present the proposed constitution. Austin wanted to refuse. Houston had stirred up the colonists to a high pitch of excitement. Let him make the long, hard trip on his own time and money. Gradually common sense overcame emotions. The settlers knew Austin. They respected his ability to deal with the Mexican authorities. Houston was admirable in many ways, but Austin knew he had a better chance of succeeding than anyone else.

With a heavy heart, Austin left for the Mexican capital on April 22, 1833. He could no longer predict what the colonists would do. He felt strongly that they should unite for Mexico.

Austin had pledged his allegiance to Mexico. He had adapted to the ways of the Mexican customs and language. The settlers looked to him for guidance. He must convince the Mexican government that the unhappy Texans only wanted to be an independent state of Mexico.

Austin was on the brink of another major decision in his life. Just as he had had to choose between his dreams and his father's, he would have to choose to which country he would pledge his loyalties. The development of Texas had become his own dream. Whatever the price he had to pay, he would remain true to that dream.

Texas must not fail!

VI

THE TEXAS REVOLUTION

Austin's trip to Mexico City was a hard one. He traveled by schooner from Matamoros to Vera Cruz. The trip took one month. Water and food became scarce. For ten days water was rationed. The only food was salt provisions. He was sick the entire trip.

After nearly three months of hardships and delays, Austin reached the capital. He was tired and sick. But he had a mission to do. The day after his arrival, he called on Mexican officials.

Santa Anna, president of Mexico, was away from the capital. Gomez Farías, vice-president, was in charge during Santa Anna's absence. Farías and other officials listened to Austin's plea for statehood for Texas. They were friendly to him. They asked him to state his plea in writing.

Austin's spirits lifted. He believed the application for statehood would be approved. He planned to be on his way back to Texas very soon.

He presented the written request on August 1, 1833. Texas wanted to be an independent state. The territory could no longer be ruled by Coahuila. On August 12, he submitted his appeal to the law which did away with

slavery. He asked that his proposals be considered with great haste.

Haste was not possible. Cholera had reached the stages of a plague in Mexico City. Congress recessed until the end of September. Austin's spirits were up and down like a seesaw. He was exhausted and ill.

Austin learned that cholera had struck the Texas settlements. Some of his family had died from the deadly disease. He was grief-stricken and desperate.

For the first time in his life, Stephen Fuller Austin acted impulsively. He wrote to the Mexican officials of San Antonio de Bexar that nothing had been done. In his opinion nothing would be done. He recommended the immediate organization of a local government for Texas as a state of the Mexican federation.

The officials at Bexar sent the letter to Farías. Farías was furious at Austin's actions. He saw the letter as a direct request for a revolution. He ordered Austin's arrest immediately.

Austin was arrested in Saltillo on January 3, 1834. He immediately wrote the Texas settlers to show no excitement about his arrest. He had committed no crime and would be found innocent. It was not in the best interests of Texas to separate from Mexico. They were to remain calm.

He was returned to Mexico City on February 13th to the old Inquisition Prison. His cell was in solitary confinement. Farías ordered that Austin was not to speak or to write to anyone.

His cell was thirteen by sixteen feet without windows. A small slot in the door admitted food. A small skylight in the ceiling offered light between the hours of ten and three. The monotony was terrible for the active man.

The first month he had no books to read. He was allowed to go to the roof for two hours a day for sunshine. He saw other prisoners but was not allowed to speak to them. His diary in which he wrote daily helped him to keep his sanity.

In April, Santa Anna resumed his duties as president. He removed the order of solitary confinement for Austin on May 9th. Austin was allowed to speak to other prisoners. He found them to be educated men who were held for political offenses. On June 12, Austin was taken to the Acordada Prison.

After eight months of imprisonment, Austin's case was assigend to the Federal District Court. His hope for freedom ended in disappointment. He wrote to friends that he hoped officials in Texas would write the government of his good character.

Texas remained silent. They took his first advice literally. They did not create excitement about his arrest. They were afraid of doing him more harm than good by speaking out for him.

Austin did not understand their silence. He was hurt at what he thought was indifference on the part of his friends. He was further distressed by rumors that people in Texas were rejoicing at his arrest.

On October 6, he was transferred to another prison, the *Carcel* of the city. His case was making no progress. No words of help or sympathy came from Texas. He had no money and thought he had no friends. He felt humiliated and defeated. He was desperate.

Texas governing bodies were not idle as Austin believed. The political chiefs met and adopted a petition for his freedom. They stated that Austin was simply the representative chosen by the convention to act in their behalf. They pleaded for his immediate release. Peter W. Grayson and Spencer H. Jackson, both lawyers, took the petition to Mexico.

Grayson and Jackson arrived on October 14th. Austin was not released on bail until Christmas Day. He was restricted to the bounds of the Federal District. Seven months passed before he was totally free.

The seven months were not wasted time for Austin. He continued to work for Texas' interest. He published "Explanation to the Public Concerning the Affairs of Texas." He worked out plans for building up trade in the Texas ports.

During that time, he lived comfortably. He made friends with educated men of affairs. He attended balls, theaters, and operas. He wrote to a friend that he was happier than he had been in fourteen years. Texas was soon to be a state and all would be well.

However, before Austin left Mexico City, he began to change his mind. Mexico was in great unrest. The United States wanted to buy Texas. He now saw the possibility of Texas belonging to the United States within two years.

Austin's return to Texas in September, 1835, was timely. Meetings were being held in all of the settlements. Conflicts were arising between those who wanted peace and those who wanted independence. Austin once again brought stability to a troubled people. He held peace or war within his hands.

"War," he decided, "is our only resource. There is no other remedy but to defend our rights, ourselves, and our country by force of arms."

Every district began gathering its militia. All reports of arms and ammunitions were to go to San Felipe, the first Texas capital. The Texans were uniting again.

Austin set up bachelor's quarters in San Felipe. His house was unfurnished. His manservant was sick. His life was devoid of physical comforts, but his home was open to all visitors.

The first battle of the Texas Revolution was in Gonzales. The Texans had a cannon. The Mexicans demanded they turn the cannon over to their army. The Texans refused. On October 2, 1835, the Texans won the first battle of the Revolution.

The Texas army gathered at Gonzales. Austin was unanimously elected to command the army. On October 12th, the march on San Antonio de Bexar was begun.

The Texas army was not one to command fear in the onlooker. Austin started his army in October with about six hundred undisciplined men. They had no oaths to bind them to service. There was no uniform to give them identity. Each man furnished his own clothes, weapons, and horse.

About one hundred and fifty of the men drifted away from the army by November. Food was scarce. Living conditions were miserable. There were no shelters from the weather. The men camped in the open air with their meager supplies.

In contrast to the dwindling Texas army, General Cós had entered Bexar. He had trained men and heavy artillery. Sam Houston was opposed to laying siege to Bexar. He was a trained military man. He had little faith in the untrained army under Austin's command. Texas lacked the power of cannons and ammunition to attack Cós.

Twice Austin submitted the question of attack to the council of war. Both times it was voted down. There was much dissatisfaction with Austin as commander-in-chief of the army. Bowie and Fannin were commanding an independent division of the army. Reports spread that Bowie was head of the army. Houston wrote to congratulate him. Fannin resigned his post, but later reconsidered.

Fannin and Houston wanted to withdraw the force which was approaching Bexar. Austin and Bowie would not do it. Restlessness and criticism ran riot in the Texas ranks. There was not enough food or clothing. No medical supplies were available. Austin authorized the Texas government to morgage all of his property for the public service.

Austin tried everything he knew to bring unity to the settlers. He appointed a committee to collect, organize, and distribute supplies. The committee fell apart. The situation was critical.

A consultation of all delegates representing the settlers was called in November. They organized a provisional government. This consisted of a governor, lieutenant governor, and a council. Henry Smith, a popular settler, was elected governor. The consultation appointed Austin, Branch T. Archer, and William H. Wharton as commissioners to the United States. Their job was to get aid and sympathy for the Texas cause.

Sam Houston was appointed commander-in-chief of the army. Houston was a respected army man. He was often emotional and abrupt. He made decisions quickly in contrast to Austin's thinking through every detail.

Austin respected Sam Houston, although they did not strongly like each other. He recognized Houston as a strong influence in the colony. He saw Houston, Bowie, and Travis as "stimulating the Texas fever" with their dreams of an empire. He knew that Houston referred to him as "the little gentleman."

Austin also knew that he had more sustaining power than Houston. He looked at everything involved before he made a decision. Once the decision was made, he went forward. Retreat was not in his vocabulary.

Cós surrendered the Alamo to Bowie and the Texas army on December 11, 1835. Many, including Sam Houston, believed the war was over. Austin knew better. War had just begun. He estimated the cost of Texas gaining its independence at several million dollars. Texans had to have help.

On December 26th, Austin, Archer, and Wharton

began their trip to the United States as commissioners of Texas. Christmas Day had been spent with friends. Austin cautioned them to remain still to ward off war as long as possible. The commissioners to the United States needed time to raise money for a navy and supplies for the army. They were to find out how the United States government felt about the Texas situation.

Austin left Texas in great despondency. He was ill from exposure in army camps. He was afraid for the future of Texas. He felt it was time for Texans to "take an open bold stand for independence."

He had left Texas out of harmony with many of his friends. He was condemned by some of his colleagues for timidity and instability. He had remained consistent in his aims—"to secure the permanent welfare of my [Austin's] people at the least suffering and sorrow to them."

Austin, Archer, and Wharton did not have immediate success in the United States. Austin and Archer were on their way back to Texas when they heard about the Battle of the Alamo. Within days of hearing the horror of the burning of all of the dead bodies at the Alamo, Austin learned of the massacre of three hundred and forty-two men at Goliad. Sam Houston had retreated. Newspapers published the story as "The Runaway Scrape." Panic-stricken people were fleeing from Texas in its moment of disaster.

"My heart and soul are sick," Austin wrote, "but my spirit is unbroken...Texas will rise again." He continued seeking donations for Texas.

Texas did rise again before Austin's return to the state in June. Houston had retreated. People were panic-stricken. But able-bodied men and boys turned out to fight. Houston's army grew daily. Shouts of "Remember the Alamo" and "Remember Goliad" resounded over the countryside.

Santa Anna became overconfident. He had the Texans on the run. The Texans did not run from San Jacinto. They were angry and ready to see blood. On April 20th, Santa Anna found Houston and his troops.

Santa Anna pitched camp. He was in no hurry. He had the Texans trapped. On April 21st, Houston held his war council: He planned to attack the Mexicans early the next morning. The men did not want to wait. They wanted to fight immediately.

The Mexicans saw the Texans coming in the late afternoon. The attack was unexpected. The Mexicans were not ready. They were not trained to fight as individuals like the frontiersmen, who came toward them with guns leveled and ready to fire.

Texas guns began to roar. Sparks and smoke filled the air. The battle took about twenty minutes. Hundreds of Mexican corpses lay on the blood-splattered field. The Texans had lost two men and thirty were wounded. The power controlling Texas had changed hands.

News of the Battle of San Jacinto flew through the country like wildfire. President Jackson wanted Texas. Austin was in Arkansas and was anxious to be back in Texas. The commissioners had secured about one hundred and twenty-five thousand dollars in loans for Texas. Many southern states sent volunteers to join the Texas army. Everywhere he went, Texas filled the air.

Austin arrived home on June 27th. In his absence, Texas had declared its indpendence. David G. Burnet was the temporary president of the Republic. A state constitution had been written. It was time for a new election of government officials. At the encouragement of friends, Austin entered the race for president.

Austin believed in his own ability to be president. He had stood by the colonists and served them faithfully. They could now show their faith in him. But would they?

Sam Houston was also a candidate for the office. Houston was the hero of the moment. Many doubts plagued Austin during the election.

Austin was surrounded by friends when a messenger came riding up, yelling, "Sam Houston is President! Sam has won!" All eyes turned to Austin.

A weak smile did not hide the hurt in his eyes. "Sam wants the same thing for Texas as I do," he said in a firm voice. "We must be united for Texas." His friends were saddened by the weary slump of his shoulders.

He did not resent Houston's victory, but he was tired. It was time to turn over the leadership of the colonists. After his defeat, Austin expressed a strong desire to be relieved of public service. Again he was a much needed man.

Houston offered him the post of secretary of state. He declined. Houston submitted his name to the Senate and he was appointed to the position. He attacked the work at hand with the same faithfulness that he had approached all duties.

Austin had never been a physically strong man. He had enjoyed few physical comforts since arriving in Texas. He had always neglected his health by overwork. His neglect was beginning to take its toll.

He continued to work long, exhausting hours. His living quarters were bare of luxuries. He had no money and his thin clothing did not protect him from the winter cold.

His friends tried to persuade him to rest. They were concerned that he often trembled with a chill. His cough was deep and hoarse. He insisted that he must continue his work.

As his own strength began to fail him, he saw strength in the harmony that was returning to his colonies. He had dreamed of the day when once again the colonies would be at peace and prosper.

Texas was approaching annexation to the United States. He had worked to encourage the union. He wanted to see Texas become a part of the United States.

Just as he had missed every dramatic episode in the history of Texas, he was not present to see his dream come true. He died on December 27, 1836, at the age of forty-three.

Austin did not have the flash, the appeal, of many who helped to shape Texas. He was frequently criticized for his work. But he was a man of deep loyalties. He made things happen. He was unrewarded in his lifetime for his faithful efforts.

He dreamed of having his own family and home on the rolling hills of the Colorado. He often expressed regret at not having his own children. He toiled endlessly for his family—Texas. The settlers were his wife and children.

He died on a pallet in an unfurnished, two-room shack. He had labored hard. He would never enjoy the fruits of his labor. He would never know that schools, colleges, and the capital of Texas would bear his name.

He would never know how many of his children whisper his name in respect and awe. But his heirs are born daily and remember—Stephen Fuller Austin, the Father of Texas.